Explore Ancient China

Zelda Wagner

Lerner Publications ◆ Minneapolis

Lerner Publications Company
An imprint of Lerner Publishing Group, Inc.
241 First Avenue North
Minneapolis, MN 55401 USA

For reading levels and more information, look up this title at www.lernerbooks.com.

Main body text set in Billy Infant Regular. Typeface provided by SparkyType.

Editor: Evan Villas **Photo Editor:** Lucien Brinkley
Lerner team: Sue Marquis

Library of Congress Cataloging-in-Publication Data

Names: Wagner, Zelda, 2000- author
Title: Explore Ancient China / Zelda Wagner.
Description: Minneapolis : Lerner Publications, [2026] | Series: Lightning Bolt Books. Early civilizations | Includes bibliographical references and index. | Audience: Ages 6-9 | Audience: Grades 2-3 | Summary: "China is one of the oldest civilizations in human history. It started more than four thousand years ago and is still thriving! Readers will discover the fascinating customs and traditions of this ancient land"— Provided by publisher.
Identifiers: LCCN 2025012284 (print) | LCCN 2025012285 (ebook) | ISBN 9798765689264 lib. bdg. | ISBN 9798348028954 pbk | ISBN 9798765696743 epub
Subjects: LCSH: China—Civilization—To 221 B.C. —Juvenile literature | China—Civilization—221 B.C.-960 A.D.—Juvenile literature | LCGFT: Literature.
Classification: LCC DS741.65 .W32 2026 (print) | LCC DS741.65 (ebook)

LC record available at https://lccn.loc.gov/2025012284
LC ebook record available at https://lccn.loc.gov/2025012285

Manufactured in the United States of America
1-1012503-54794-5/13/2025

Table of Contents

The Ancient Chinese

Ancient China began more than four thousand years ago. It was one of the world's first civilizations.

Ancient China was in East Asia. It lay in the eastern part of modern China.

Two rivers divided ancient China. People farmed along the Yellow River. They fished in the Yangtze River.

Powerful families called dynasties ruled the land. The same family stayed in power for many years.

A painting of Yu the Great, a Chinese ruler from old stories

Ancient China
Ancient China
River
ASIA
Yellow River
Yangtze River
YELLOW SEA
PACIFIC OCEAN

Life in Ancient China

Everyone in ancient China had a role. The biggest group was the peasants. They farmed the land.

Craftspeople made pottery, chariots, and weapons. Merchants sold goods. Nobles ruled the cities, states, and villages.

Ancient Chinese pottery

Ancient Chinese writing used characters instead of letters.

People spoke an old form of the Chinese language. It was written from top to bottom on animal bones or scrolls made from bamboo or silk.

People honored the gods with statues.

The ancient Chinese had many gods. There were gods of the sun, moon, and wind. There were water, soil, and other gods too.

The ancient Chinese invented silk fabric, strong boats, and kites. They made cups, animal figures, and swords out of bronze.

This bronze goose was carved about three thousand years ago.

Early Chinese people made clay vases and pots. They carved necklaces and knives from jade.

This hare is made of jade.

Festivals took place throughout the year. The most important was the spring festival, or Chinese New Year. It is celebrated at the end of winter.

Imperial China

The last five hundred years of ancient China were a time of war. The Chinese states fought one another to control the land.

Soldiers fought on horseback. The war raged until about two thousand years ago.

Horses pulled large chariots into battle.

The state of Qin won the war. Qin united all of China under one dynasty for the first time.

When the emperor of Qin died, he was buried with eight thousand statues of soldiers.

This event marked the end of ancient China and the beginning of Imperial China.

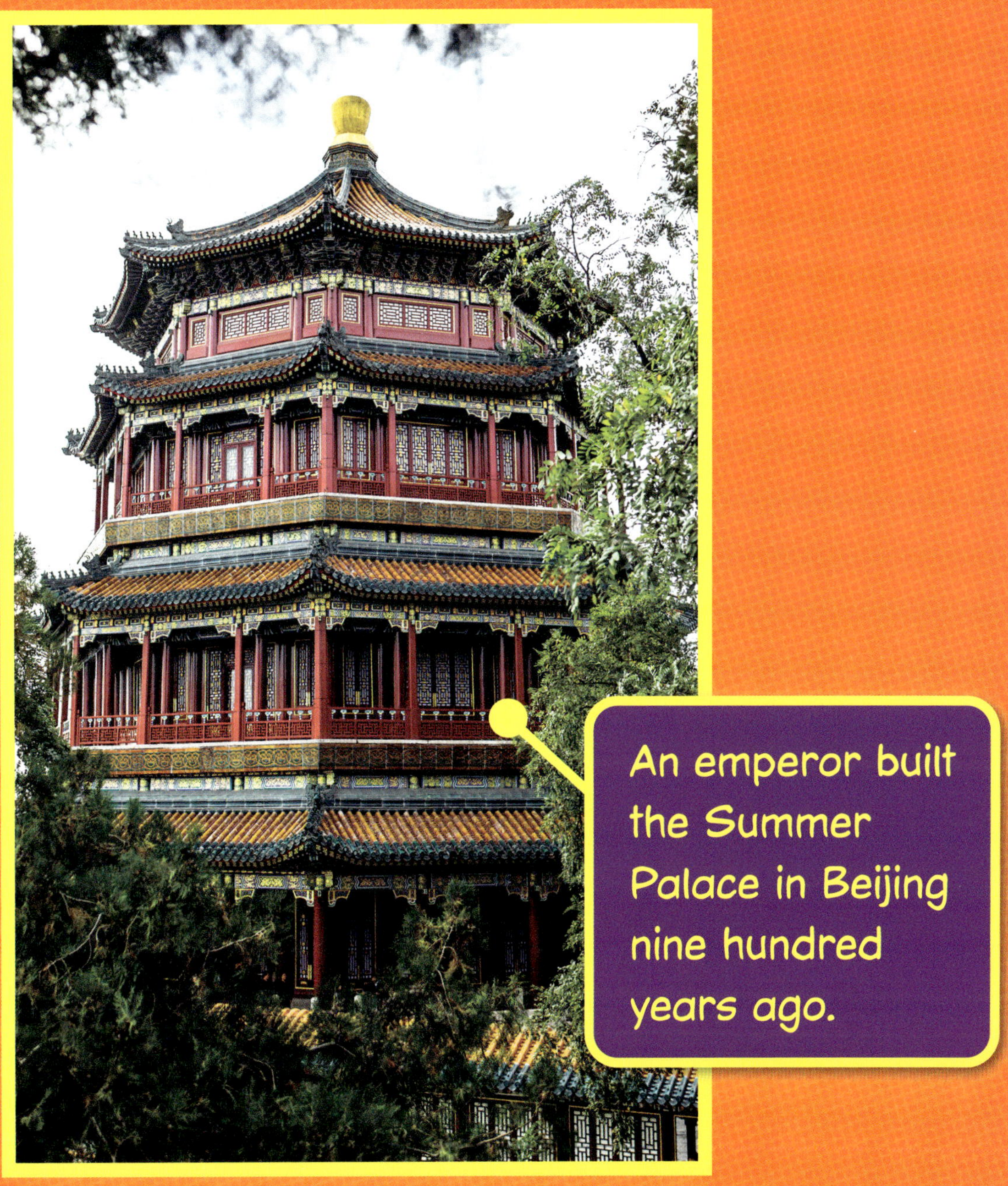

An emperor built the Summer Palace in Beijing nine hundred years ago.

A Look at Ancient Chinese Markets

Each village had its own market. This was the center of village life. On market day, a noble raised a flag to signal that the market was open. Villagers bought food, pottery, and cloth. Children played with their friends. Adults chatted with neighbors. They shared information about what was happening in their village.

Ancient China Facts

- Some ancient Chinese nobles used "dragon bones" to talk to the gods. These bones came from cows or turtles.
- The ancient Chinese created calendars based on the movement of the moon.
- The Zhou were the longest-ruling dynasty in ancient China. They ruled for almost eight hundred years.

Glossary

bronze: metal made of copper and tin

chariot: a vehicle pulled by horses and used in ancient war

civilization: a large group of people who share a culture

dynasty: a family that rules for many years

jade: a hard green gemstone

merchant: a buyer and seller of goods

noble: a person of high social rank

peasant: a farmer of low social rank

Learn More

Britannica Kids: China
https://kids.britannica.com/kids/article/China/345666

Ducksters: Ancient China for Kids
https://www.ducksters.com/history/china/ancient_china.php

Faust, D. R. *The Rise and Fall of Ancient China.* Bearport, 2025.

Havemeyer, Janie. *A Day in Ancient China.* Jump!, 2025.

History for Kids: Chinese Daily Life
https://www.historyforkids.net/ancient-chinese-daily-life.html

Ransom, Candice. *Explore Ancient India*. Lerner Publications, 2026.

Index

Photo Acknowledgments

Image credits: Jerry Jian/Getty Images, p. 4; DuKai photographer/Getty Images, p. 5; CHAO-FENG LIN/Getty Images, p. 6; Ma Lin, Public Domain, p. 7; Laura Westlund/Independent Picture Service, p. 8; xiaokebetter/Getty Images, p. 9; Heritage Image Partnership Ltd/Alamy, p. 10; Xiao Yijiu/Xinhua via Getty Images, p. 11; Richard I'Anson/Getty Images, p. 12; Gary L. Todd, Ph.D., Professor of History, Sias International University, Xinzheng, China, p. 13; yipengge/Getty Images, p. 14; Carles Navarro Parcerisas/Getty Images, p. 15; Charlie & Melody Wambeke (CC BY-SA 2.0), p. 16; Zossolino (CC BY-SA 4.0), p. 17; QINQIE99/Shutterstock, p. 18; Maremagnum/Getty Images, p. 19; Artist Unknown, Public Domain, p. 20.

Cover: iannomadav/Getty Images.